SUPERCARS

ASTON MARTIN

Ryan Smith

AV2

www.av2books.com

Step 1
Go to **www.av2books.com**

Step 2
Enter this unique code

JQDOGPJ64

Step 3
Explore your interactive eBook!

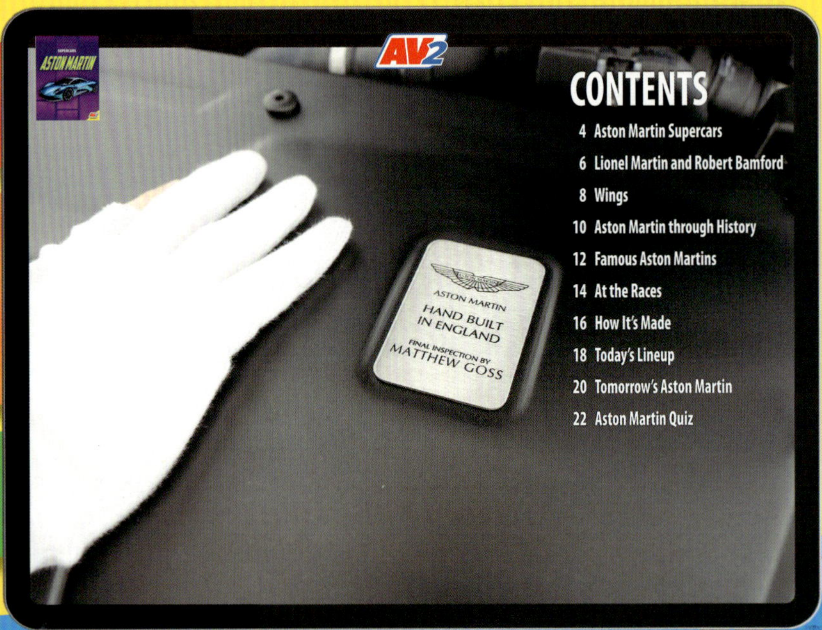

AV2 is optimized for use on any device

Your interactive eBook comes with...

Contents
Browse a live contents page to easily navigate through resources

Audio
Listen to sections of the book read aloud

Videos
Watch informative video clips

Weblinks
Gain additional information for research

Try This!
Complete activities and hands-on experiments

Key Words
Study vocabulary, and complete a matching word activity

Quizzes
Test your knowledge

Slideshows
View images and captions

... and much, much more!

View new titles and product videos at www.av2books.com

SUPERCARS

ASTON MARTIN

CONTENTS

ASTON

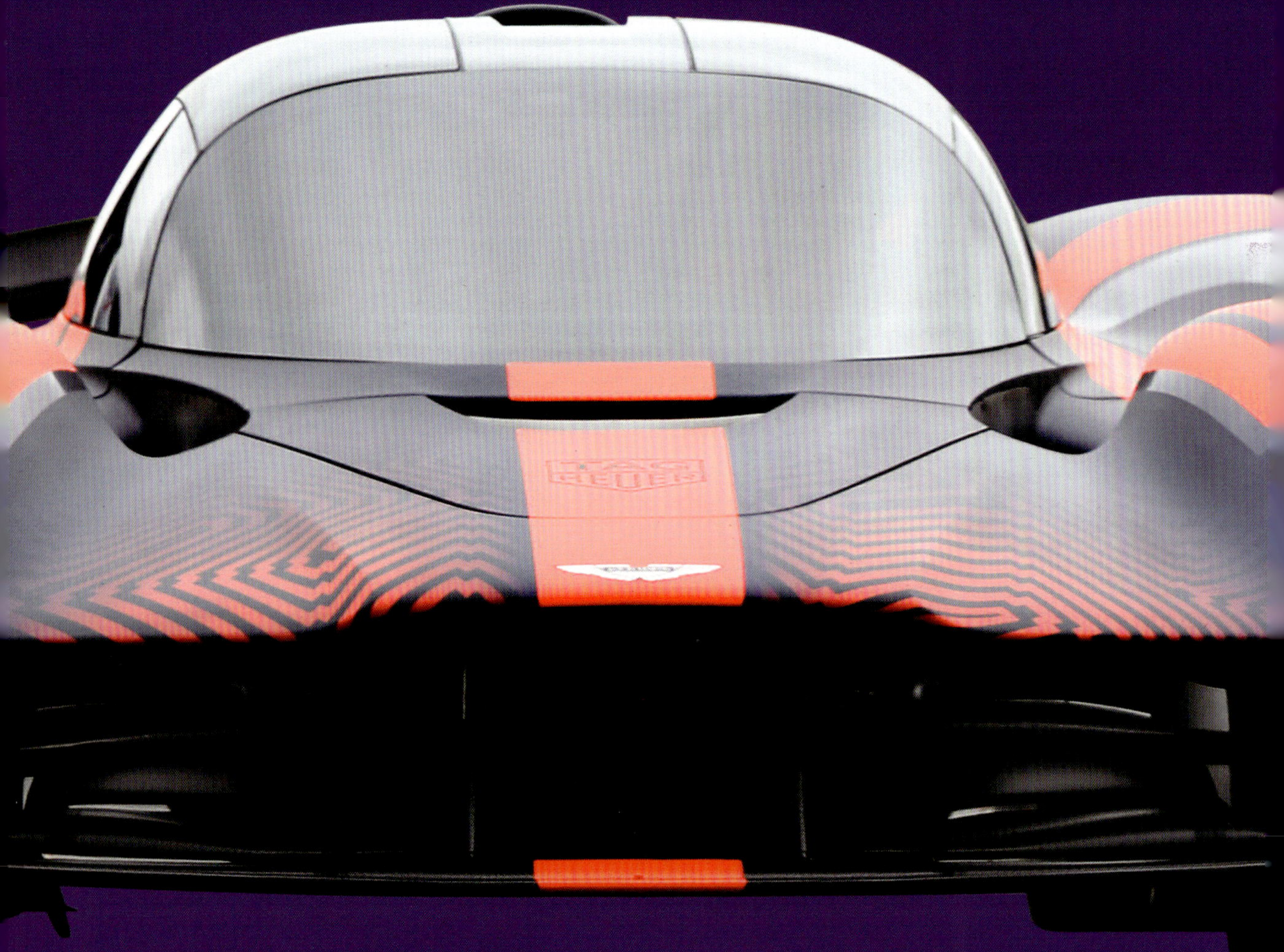

MARTIN

ASTON MARTIN SUPERCARS

A supercar is more than just a really fast sports car. It is also far more **luxurious** than a sports car. Great care is taken when a supercar is built. Every detail must be perfect before one of these cars can go to a customer. Such high quality standards mean that only so many supercars are built each year. It also means that the price tag for a supercar starts at hundreds of thousands of dollars.

As of **2019**, fewer than **90,000** Aston Martins have been built.

Aston Martin is one of the best-known supercar companies in the United Kingdom. For more than 100 years, Aston Martin has been making luxurious supercars that look like works of art and have the power of a race car.

An **Aston Martin DBR1** sold for **$22.5 million** in **2017**.

LIONEL MARTIN AND ROBERT BAMFORD

Lionel Martin was a car **enthusiast** and race car driver. Robert Bamford was an **engineer**. The two friends started out as car salesmen. In 1913, they decided to start their own car-building company. They wanted to make cars that were fast and beautiful.

Lionel and Robert first called their company Bamford & Martin Ltd. In 1914, they changed the name to Aston Martin after Lionel won the Aston Hill Climb in one of their cars. Hill climbs were events that tested a car's **performance**.

Aston Martin continued to find success in hill climb events.

MAP OF THE UNITED KINGDOM

At the top of the hill where the Aston Hill Climb took place stands the Aston Martin Monument. It was built to remember Lionel's success in the event.

WINGS

Aston Martin has one of the best-known car logos. The very first Aston Martin logo was a circle with an A and M in the middle. Aston Martin changed its logo to a pair of eagle wings in 1927. Since then, the logo has only had changes to its color and shape.

The A and M logo was used on Aston Martin cars from 1921 to 1926.

ASTON MARTIN LOGO

The colors of the wings represent elegance and excellence.

The eagle wings symbolize speed and agility.

The green color represents Aston Martin's commitment to an environmentally friendly future.

ASTON MARTIN THROUGH HISTORY

Lionel and Robert wanted to make beautiful sports cars. Today, Aston Martin is one of the most iconic luxury car brands in the world.

Aston Martin takes part in its first **Formula 1 (F1)** race. The company continues to take part in F1 races until the end of the 1960 season.

1914

1947

1959

Lionel Martin and Robert Bamford build their first car, the Coal Scuttle.

David Brown buys Aston Martin. He produces the DB series of cars during his time with the company.

1987

The Ford Motor Company buys Aston Martin. Ford sells Aston Martin in 2007.

2018

Aston Martin becomes a **publicly traded company**.

2020

Aston Martin releases its first SUV, the Aston Martin DBX.

FAMOUS ASTON MARTINS

Aston Martin is well-known for being the car driven by the fictional spy James Bond. Bond first drove an Aston Martin DB5 loaded with spy gadgets in the movie *Goldfinger*. From 1964 to 2020, Aston Martin **models** have appeared in 12 James Bond movies.

The spy gadgets in James Bond's DB5 include tire slashers, oil slicks, and ejector seats.

The 25th James Bond movie, *No Time to Die*, features four different Aston Martins. The DB5 makes its seventh appearance in a James Bond movie. The Aston Martin V8 Saloon, the Aston Martin DBS Superleggera, and the Aston Martin Valhalla also make appearances in *No Time to Die*.

Aston Martin Valhalla

Aston Martin V8 Saloon

Aston Martin Superleggera

AT THE RACES

Today's Aston Martin race team was founded in 2005. It is called Aston Martin Racing. The team races different models of the Aston Martin Vantage. Aston Martin Racing takes part in race series around the world, including the FIA World Endurance Championship and the Avon Tyres British GT Championship.

In 2018, Aston Martin began to make a return to Formula 1 racing. It became the main sponsor of the Red Bull Racing team. Starting in 2021, Aston Martin will have its own F1 team. 2021 will mark 61 years since Aston Martin had its own team in a Formula 1 race.

Driving an Aston Martin Vantage in 2015, Jamie Chadwick became the first woman and youngest person to win the British GT Championship.

Aston Martin Racing won the Petit Le Mans endurance race in 2006.

Aston Martin Racing took part in the Rolex 24 at Daytona endurance race in 2020.

Aston Martin has entered **more than 4,000 races**.

As of 2019, Aston Martin Racing has won the **24 Hours of Le Mans** endurance race **4 times**.

Red Bull Racing won three races in 2019.

HOW IT'S MADE

The main Aston Martin factory is in Gaydon, England. The company has another factory in St Athan, Wales. Every Aston Martin is **assembled** by hand. Most car companies start building a new car every few seconds. Aston Martin starts a new car every 26 minutes. Every detail has to be just right before a car can move to the next step on the assembly line.

Aston Martin's main factory sits on 54 acres (22 hectares) of land.

Technicians install more than 10,000 parts onto an Aston Martin.

It takes about **200 hours** to build an Aston Martin.

Aston Martin makes more than **6,000 cars** a year.

Each technician is in charge of a certain task on the assembly line.

Every detail of each Aston Martin is closely inspected before the car leaves the factory.

TODAY'S LINEUP

Aston Martin models present luxury and performance in new and exciting ways. Today's Aston Martins can be customized to make each car unique to each customer.

The Aston Martin Valkyrie is the company's first **hypercar**. Driving a Valkyrie is meant to feel like driving a Formula 1 race car. The DBX expands Aston Martin into the everyday driving market. It will help Aston Martin meet the needs of even more customers with its increased seating and storage space.

Here are some of the Aston Martins on the road today.

Aston Martin Vantage Coupe

Engine: **V8**

Maximum Horsepower: **503**

0–60 mph (0–100 km/h): **3.6 seconds**

Starting Price: **$156,081**

Aston Martin DBX

Engine: **V8**

Maximum Horsepower: **542**

0–60 mph (0–100 km/h): **4.5 seconds**

Starting Price: **$192,086**

Aston Martin Rapide AMR

Engine: **V12**

Maximum Horsepower: **595**

0–60 mph (0–100 km/h): **4.2 seconds**

Starting Price: **$207,775**

Aston Martin DB11 AMR

Engine: **V12**

Maximum Horsepower: **630**

0–60 mph (0–100 km/h): **3.7 seconds**

Starting Price: **$250,000**

Aston Martin DBS Superleggera Volante

Engine: **V12**

Maximum Horsepower: **715**

0–60 mph (0–100 km/h): **3.4 seconds**

Starting Price: **$307,820**

Aston Martin Valkyrie

Engine: **V12**

Maximum Horsepower: **1,160**

0–60 mph (0–100 km/h): **2.3 seconds**

Starting Price: **$3,000,000**

TOMORROW'S ASTON MARTIN

Aston Martin has big plans for the future. From more supercars to personal air travel, Aston Martin is looking for new ways to improve luxury travel.

Aston Martin's newest **concept car** is the Vanquish Vision Concept. This supercar will be built from materials that will make it lighter and faster than previous Aston Martins.

Aston Martin is preparing for the future of personal flight with its Volante Vision Concept. The Volante Vision Concept will be able to fly itself to different places throughout a city. Its passengers will avoid the traffic on the ground.

The Vanquish Vision Concept has cameras instead of sideview mirrors.

The design of the Vanquish Vision Concept is inspired by the Valkyrie.

The Vanquish will go on sale in 2022.

The Volante Vision Concept will seat three passengers.

ASTON MARTIN QUIZ

1 As of 2019, how many Aston Martins have been built?

2 In what year did Lionel Martin and Robert Bamford decide to start their own car-building company?

3 What do the eagle wings in the Aston Martin logo symbolize?

4 What was the first Aston Martin car called?

5 How many Aston Martins are in the James Bond movie *No Time to Die*?

6 Aston Martin has entered how many races?

7 How long does it take to build an Aston Martin?

8 Which Aston Martin is the company's first SUV?

9 What is the starting price of the Aston Martin Valkyrie?

10 How will the Volante Vision Concept help its passengers avoid traffic?

ANSWERS

1 Fewer than 90,000 **2** 1913 **3** Speed and agility **4** The Coal Scuttle **5** Four **6** More than 4,000 **7** About 200 hours **8** The Aston Martin DBX **9** $3,000,000 **10** It will fly over the city

KEY WORDS

assembled: put together

concept car: a car built to show off new technologies and designs

engineer: a person trained in how to build things and use different materials

enthusiast: someone who is very interested or involved in something

Formula 1 (F1): the highest level of single-seat car racing

hypercar: a car that is even faster, more exclusive, and more luxurious than a supercar

luxurious: something that is pleasing, comfortable, and expensive

models: the different car designs made by a company

performance: how well something does its intended task

publicly traded company: a company that sells its shares to the general public

INDEX

Get the best of both worlds.

AV2 bridges the gap between print and digital.

The expandable resources toolbar enables quick access to content including **videos**, **audio**, **activities**, **weblinks**, **slideshows**, **quizzes**, and **key words**.

Animated videos make static images come alive.

Resource icons on each page help readers to further **explore key concepts**.

Published by AV2
14 Penn Plaza, 9th Floor
New York, NY 10122
Website: www.av2books.com

Library of Congress Cataloging-in-Publication Data

Names: Smith, Ryan, author.
Title: Aston Martin / Ryan Smith.
Description: New York, NY : AV2, [2021] | Series: Supercars | Includes index. | Audience: Ages 8-12. | Audience: Grades 4-6.
Identifiers: LCCN 2020016890 (print) | LCCN 2020016891 (ebook) | ISBN 9781791125714 (library binding) | ISBN 9781791125721 (paperback) | ISBN 9781791125738 | ISBN 9781791125745
Subjects: LCSH: Aston Martin automobile--Juvenile literature.
Classification: LCC TL215.A75 S45 2020 (print) | LCC TL215.A75 (ebook) | DDC 629.222--dc23
LC record available at https://lccn.loc.gov/2020016890
LC ebook record available at https://lccn.loc.gov/2020016891

Printed in Guangzhou, China
1 2 3 4 5 6 7 8 9 0 24 23 22 21 20

062020
101119

Art Director: Terry Paulhus Project Coordinator: Ryan Smith

The publisher acknowledges Alamy, Getty Images, and Shutterstock as its primary image suppliers for this title.